THANK YOU
GOD
THANK YOU
JESUS

THANK YOU
GOD
THANK YOU
JESUS

THE STORY OF
VU (VICTOR) PHAM

HIS AMAZING SURVIVAL AND
TRANSITION BY THE GRACE OF GOD
AND THE FORGIVENESS OF JESUS.

KONNIE MEYER

XULON PRESS

Xulon Press
2301 Lucien Way #415
Maitland, FL 32751
407.339.4217
www.xulonpress.com

Unless otherwise indicated, Scripture quotations taken from the Holy Bible, New International Version (NIV). Copyright © 1973, 1978, 1984, 2011 by Biblica, Inc.™. Used by permission. All rights reserved.

Printed in the United States of America.

ISBN-13: 978-1-54567-198-6

TABLE OF CONTENTS

-GENESIS-
IN THE BEGINNING

Thirteen years ago, when we first met, I was in the salon to have my nails done. My first impression of Victor (Vu) was, he's this bubbly Asian guy with a big smile and piercing dark eyes. I'm guessing he saw me as this uptight, white lady with gray hair and nails that needed a lot of work.

So, at first glance, the following chapters might seem to be an unlikely collaboration between two very different people-people from totally opposite backgrounds. Vu, the subject of this book, is a Vietnamese refugee, former gun toting gang member, one time drug dealer and addict turned youth advocate and businessman. As for myself, the author, I'm a farm wife, retired teacher, part-time writer, mother and grandmother.

For as long as I've known him, Victor was never shy about sharing his belief in God and Jesus. Being raised a Missouri Synod Lutheran I, on the other hand, was taught to be distrustful of anyone who "wore religion on their sleeve."

Time progresses and our differences melt away. Then comes the realization we share one very important similarity. We both sincerely believe, with the help of God and the forgiveness of Jesus, all things are possible. Just maybe this isn't such an odd collaboration after all.

Victor and I hope you enjoy reading his true life's story.

FOREWORD

The United States withdrew its troops from South Vietnam in 1975. The years that followed marked a period of great uncertainty and unrest for the people living in that region as the Communist Party, backed by the North Vietnamese Army and Viet Cong guerrilla forces, gained control.

It's estimated over two million Vietnamese died as a result of starvation, torture, illness, and over-work. In order to escape these harsh conditions, many Vietnamese risked their lives and fled their country by boat. As a result, thousands upon thousands more died at sea. But those who survived lived through some remarkable transitions. Vu Pham's experience is one such story.

Born in 1977, in a small village in South Vietnam, Vu Pham's life begins during this time of social, civil, and political upheaval. In the following pages, Vu speaks to you, the reader, sharing his incredible life's

Thank You God. Thank You Jesus.

story. I am honored and humbled to be part of this retelling process.

Konnie Meyer

April 15, 2019

Hamler, Ohio

PART 1

INTO THE
UNKNOWN

CHAPTER 1

Looking at his disciples, he said: Blessed are you who are poor, for yours is the kingdom of God. Blessed are you who hunger now, for you will be satisfied. Blessed are you who weep now, for you will laugh. — Luke 6: 20 - 21

There's no one around to help me. Everyone must be busy or resting after a long afternoon working in the rice fields. As for me, I am hungry. My mother says I'm always hungry. What she says is true, which is probably why I want a banana. The bananas grow on our tree in the side yard. Mother always puts bunches of them in a special dark place. I can't reach the top shelf of this place in our outdoor shed. Even if I stand on my tiptoes, I cannot reach that high.

Everyone says for being five years old I am small for my age. My mother says I make up for my size by

3

having double the energy. She's right. She also says I get into double the trouble. That's because I like to do things; I like to keep busy. I look around. There's nothing to stand on, but this does not stop me. I climb up the shelf, gripping with my fingers and toes.

It's a good thing I don't have any shoes because this makes it easier to keep my balance while climbing. My fingers can almost touch the smooth skin of the yellow prize. My mouth begins to water just thinking about its sweet flavor. I let go of the shelf to reach with my right hand, but I feel myself slip. Losing my balance I fall, landing on my shoulder. I cry out. My father scoops me up in his arms. If something in my arm or shoulder is broken or torn, there is very little anyone can do since we have no doctor or hospital close by. Father says my shoulder must heal on its own.

Our village is poor. We have no running water or electricity. The people in our village do not have much food. Everyone eats the same thing: rice, bananas, a few vegetables, and fish. Sometimes at night I hear my parents talk. They are worried about this group of bad people they call the Viet Cong coming into our village. They worry things will get worse. I hear them say when this happens, no one will be safe.

Together, twice a day, our family walks down a dusty road to our church. We get up in the dark so we can be there by four in the morning. Again, we go to church in the late afternoon. Grandmother joins us along the way. The church is one small room with benches. We sit with other people from our village.

Up front there's a statue of a man named Jesus. His hair is long and brown. He has a beard. He's on a cross. His hands and feet have nails through them. I see red where the nails are. His head is hanging down. On top of his head are many twisted sticks with sharp thorns. There's red on his head around the thorns too. His face looks sad.

When the priest is talking, I stare at this statue and think to myself, *This man must be brave because thorns and nails hurt.* Mother says He is God's son. She says He died on the cross, so when we ask for forgiveness for the bad things we've done, called sins, God will forgive us. I know I sometimes do bad things, so I'm glad to hear this.

My grandmother lives close by, this is why she walks with us to church. Since Grandfather died, she lives alone. On one occasion, she invites me to stay overnight at her house. Everything is dark. There are no street lights or lights in the house. In this darkness, men break into my grandmother's house. They beat my grandmother and steal what little she has.

During all this I hear nothing, and I don't wake up. In the morning, I find out about the robbery and the attack on Grandmother. She has bruises and cuts. Her eyes are red from crying. I feel bad. I feel guilty for not waking up to help her. If I had been awake, I could have gotten someone to come.

After what happened to Grandmother, Mother and Father whisper even more. They think all their children are asleep, but I cannot sleep, so I listen. Their talk frightens me. I'm scared of what will happen if more of these bad men come into our town. I don't want our family to leave like so many others. I wish everything to be just like it is, forever.

Almost one year later, I learn wishing does not make it so. The way things are and the way I want them to be are two different things. My life soon changes, forever.

CHAPTER 2

Be strong and take heart, all you who
hope in the Lord. — Psalms 31: 24

Last night, my older brother, Giang, and I were
smuggled onto a fishing boat. He told me we are on
an ocean. All I know is, it is a new day and I am not
at home. I'm on a boat with my brother and eighteen
strangers. Everywhere I look I see blue. When I look up,
I see blue sky. When I look down, I see blue water. In my
six years of life, my eyes have never seen so many different shades of the same color in one place. I wonder,
How is this even possible? Then again I wonder, *Does
my eight year old brother notice this too?*

I look over at him. His eyes are closed. He doesn't
open them. I'm not sure if he is really sleeping or just
keeping his eyes shut while he thinks about yesterday.
It was a long day and a scary day. It was also a sad one

for both of us. I don't want to bother him, so I just look instead.

If he's closing his eyes to think, what is he thinking about? I study his face, trying to guess. Maybe he's missing our family and the home we left behind. Maybe he wishes he could have said good-by to our father and mother. It is also possible Giang is not thinking anything. It is early morning. Perhaps he is so tired he is simply sleeping.

Since we left home, Giang has been very quiet. He has never been talkative, but all day yesterday he did not speak a single word as our father walked with us from our small village of Kinh 7b Khu 3 to that distant place, that town with so many noisy cars, bikes, and people. It was then, when two strangers, men dressed in black, riding black motorcycles, wearing black helmets, took us away from our father, away from everything we had ever known.

I recall how it happened on that narrow street with buildings on both sides. For a short time, the three of us stood together in silence, waiting. Then suddenly, from around the corner, two men on bikes appear and pull up beside us. They do not get off. My father nods at the drivers and hands them something from his pocket.

8

As if Giang already knows what to do, he climbs on back of the first bike. The stranger on the second bike grabs my arm, pulling me up hard onto the back. Tightly, I grip his shirt with my fingers. I don't want to fall off, and I don't want to wrap my arms around this person I do not know.

I remember looking at my father, seeing my reflection in the liquid pool of his sad eyes. I'm afraid, but I try to act brave like Giang or that image of Jesus back home in our church. As we ride away with the strangers, I quickly turn my head. Looking back, I cry out to Father. I want to see him, I need to see him, but he is not there. Our father is gone!

These smugglers take us to the edge of the world, that place where the land and the water come together. We get off the bikes and follow them onto a rickety, wooden dock. They tell us we are going to sneak onto a boat, so we must be quiet. By now it is dark. There is a chill in the air. The sun is gone, making it hard to see.

We all crouch down, trying not to draw attention, trying not to make a sound. The smugglers lead the way. Giang and I do not have shoes, and I can feel the uneven boards beneath my feet. I am afraid I might stumble and fall into the water, so I hold on tight to my brother's hand.

At the end of the dock there is a boat waiting for us. It is bobbing in the water, but a rope looped around a post keeps it in place, keeps it from drifting away. By the moonlight, my brother and I strain our eyes to see into the boat. It is full of strangers. Giang whispers, "Vu, there's room here!" He points to a narrow space where no one is sitting.

A few people move aside so we can climb on board. An older woman reaches up to steady me as Giang and I carefully step down into this small, crowded fishing boat. The two smugglers do not follow us. They stay behind, removing the rope from the post. As soon as we sit down, someone starts the engine. Whether we like it or not, from this point forward, the two of us are headed into the unknown.

CHAPTER 3

When he reached a certain place, he stopped for the night because the sun had set. Taking one of the stones there, he put it under his head and lay down to sleep. — Genesis 28: 11

The boat moves into the shadowy darkness. I have an empty feeling in the pit of my stomach. Everything familiar is gone. I feel like crying, but I know I must not, so instead I cling to my brother. Huddled together, we sit in our tiny space on this boat, which is now our home.

Giang and I lean our heads back, against the side of the boat to rest. There's very little room, so we sit with our legs bent. I don't like it here. It doesn't feel good to be here. The deck of the boat is wet and hard. My body aches from that long walk with our father. This is our first night away from home. I miss my mom, I miss my family, I miss my bed. I worry, *How many more nights will we be here on this crowded boat?* I am afraid to fall asleep surrounded by so much deep, dark water, but my eyes feel heavy. I can no longer keep them open.

When I awake, I see the bright morning sun. At first, I feel afraid, I don't know where I am. Then I remember last night. Everywhere I look I see blue. I look up and see blue sky. I look down and see blue water. I look over at Giang. His eyes are closed. He doesn't open them.

By afternoon our boat is out of gas. We are drifting without direction. The sound of the motor has gone silent. What I mostly hear now are waves hitting the sides of the boat. It is a soft sound. If a wave is big, it makes our boat rock. Then the water splashes over the sides making our hair, skin, and clothes wet. Some of the people talk, but they talk softly. Sometimes I hear a cough or a groan. Sometimes I see a bird fly overhead, but I cannot hear it fly.

When I look around, everyone seems to be quietly thinking their own thoughts. Their faces aren't happy or sad. They are the blank faces of strangers; strangers with no expressions, hiding their fear. I wish Giang would talk. I wish he did not have that same blank look on his face as the strangers, I wish....

Now, two full days have passed since we began clinging like ants to this floating leaf that is our boat. There is no food. We ran out of what little we had yesterday. At least ants can nibble at their leaf, but we have nothing. Even if Giang and I don't talk much, I can hear our stomachs talking to each other. They are saying, "We want food! We need food!" My stomach hurts. Giang says his stomach hurts too. I wonder what will happen if we don't find something to eat.

After three full days, we are still drifting aimlessly with no land in sight. Our water supply is also gone. Once, when I leaned over the side of the boat to scoop up a handful of water, my brother took ahold of my arm and stopped me. He said, "No, Vu! You cannot drink from the ocean. It will make you sick. It is full of salt."

I think he is right. I can tell when the water splashes over the side of our boat it's different from water in the stream near our house. It's different from the water in the rice paddies where my family and everyone in the village works. Also, I know it is different because when I lick my lips, they taste like salt. I even lick my arm and it too tastes salty.

There is salt in my hair, in my eyebrows, in my ears, in my nose, and there is salt in between my toes. Here we are, in the middle of so much water, yet we cannot drink. I don't like this blue water with so much salt. My mouth is dry. I'm so thirsty! My stomach hurts. I am so hungry! I am so very tired of being on this crowded boat! All I want is to go back home, but I know this is not possible, so I sit with my arms wrapped around my knees, watching the sun slowly disappear behind the ocean.

CHAPTER 4

Do not forget to entertain strangers, for by so doing some people have entertained angels without knowing it. — Hebrew 13: 2

This is our fourth night bobbing helplessly in the darkness, as once again the light-blue of the day-time sky is replaced by the blackish-blue of the night-time sky. So much empty space scares me, but I push back my tears. When I look up at the stars, I feel better. Having a blanket would help me feel better too.

My brother and I are wearing shorts and T-shirts. They're the same clothes we wear every day. They are the only clothes we own. When we were home and our clothes got dirty, we washed them on the rocks in the stream. The night air is cool. Our clothes do not keep us warm, so I move closer to my brother. The moon is bright. It glows, but its glow doesn't keep me warm the way the sun's glow does.

The dark sky is full of many little twinkling stars. I wonder if my baby brother and two sisters see the same stars I see. I wonder if my mother, father, and grandmother also see these same stars. The small white specks in the sky make me think of the grains of rice that fill our clay bowls for almost every meal.

I can close my eyes and smell the rice cooking on my mother's open fire. I can picture all of my family sitting together on the floor of our two-room house with a thatched roof, eating with chop sticks, savoring the rice my mother prepared. Thinking about rice makes my mouth water. It makes my stomach growl.

I hear people on the boat whispering. They say we're all going to die here on this ocean. They say without food or water we cannot live for many more days. I think about walking twice a day, in the early morning and late afternoon, with my family to our little church down the road. It is at this church where I hear the story about how God saves His people in the wilderness by sending manna from the sky to feed them. I pray God helps us like He helped those people in the Bible.

When I open my eyes at sunrise, I'm surprised to see a boat drifting beside ours. It's full of men, men with guns, scary looking men. Someone once told me stories about pirates that took what they wanted, killed the passengers, and sank their ship. My heart beats fast. I can feel it pounding inside my chest. I huddle even closer to Giang. I brace myself against my brother. He whispers in my ear to be still and say nothing. I do not think I could say a word, even if I tried.

Squinting, with the sun in my eyes, I stare at the tallest, meanest looking man. I think he is the leader. I see a scar on his face. He stands with his legs apart, the sun to his back. Blocking the sun's glare with my hand, I keep my eyes on him. His hand is on a shiny weapon at his side. His finger is on the pistol's trigger. Our eyes meet. I feel his dark eyes peering directly into my eyes, into my soul. He stands there staring, looking only at me, not moving, doing nothing for a few seconds.

Then he does something unexpected. Taking his finger off the trigger, he removes his hand from the weapon. Next, he leans over. Lifting a flat, round lid with one hand, he reaches into the now open wooden barrel with the other. As he stands up, he tosses us handfuls of burned rice! He orders two other men to do the same.

17

We frantically compete for the life-saving food, catching whatever we can, shoving it into our mouths. The pirate ship leaves, but we all spend many minutes picking hungrily at the tiny, missed grains of rice that have fallen on the deck. I believe this rice is our manna sent from God. We will survive another day. *Thank you, God!*

CHAPTER 5

So do not fear, for I am with you; do not be dismayed, for I am your God. I will strengthen you and help you; I will uphold you with my righteous right hand. — Isaiah 41: 10

There's nothing anyone can do on this fishing boat but think, sleep, and worry. I think about my family. It becomes a game. I try to guess what everyone is doing at home. Are my sisters walking down the dirt road toward school? When they arrive, does the priest ask, "Where is Vu? Where is Giang?" Does he want to know what has become of my brother and me? Do the nuns who teach us ask my sisters any questions? Do the other students want to know why we are not in school? I wonder if anyone is thinking about us. I wonder if anyone cares. I wonder if they miss me as much as I miss them.

This is our fifth night at sea. I know this is so because I counted each night, using all five fingers on one hand. When I close my eyes to sleep, I see pictures in my head, pictures of home, pictures of my family before we went away. I see my little brother, Tao. Together we search for sticks. When we each find one, we sit at the edge of the road drawing pictures in the dirt. If we don't like what we draw, we rub our hands across the pictures, and like magic they disappear.

In my dream, I see Giang. We kick a ball back and forth to each other. He bends down to pick it up. He acts like he is going to throw it across the roof of our house. When I see what he is about to do, I run to the other side and catch it. Then we walk to the stream near our house. We each pick up a handful of pebbles and toss them into the water, one at a time as hard as we can, trying to see which one makes the biggest splash.

Through the fog of dreams and sleep I hear the muffled sound of people talking, stirring. Giang pokes me in the side with his elbow. He tells me, "Vu, hurry, and wake up!" When I open my eyes to this new day, I rub them. Then, in the distance, I see a tiny brown speck bobbing on top of the blue water against the blue sky. I narrow my eyes, trying to figure out what is coming our way. Everyone silently looks in the same direction, straining their eyes to see what is out there on the horizon.

People begin to point. Nervously, we watch and wait as the tiny object moves slowly toward us, growing in size as it gets closer. Nobody says it out loud, but we are all afraid. We are afraid because we know this floating object could be another pirate ship heading our way.

If it is what we fear, we also know this next time we might not be so lucky. I worry if it's a pirate ship, I may never see my family again. I don't want to die here today, on the bottom of this salty, blue ocean with all of these strangers. I don't want any of us to die at the hands of pirates.

There's a Bible story I remember from school. It tells about a boy named David who bravely challenges Goliath, a giant. With God's help, David wins the battle by killing the giant. I want to be like David. If the pirates come back, I'll be just as brave as he was. I'll ask God to help me. If they try to hurt my brother and me, I'll be ready to fight! Just like David, I will win the battle.

CHAPTER 6

When Pharaoh's horses, chariots, and horsemen went into the sea, the Lord brought the waters of the sea back over them, but the Israelites walked through the sea on dry ground. — Exodus 15: 19

For many minutes I keep my eyes focused, looking into the distance. Time passes. As the object gets closer, my eyes tell me I will not have to fight like David, because the object I see does not appear to be a pirate ship. Once everyone on our fishing boat realizes there's nothing to fear, tears of joy mix with cheers of thanksgiving.

We all welcome the large, ocean, rescue ship coming to save us from certain death. One at a time, twenty tired, dirty, thirsty, and hungry refugees, including Giang and myself, are helped on board. It feels good to be

23

able to stand up and stretch. On this rescue ship, we're given much needed food and water.

The ship takes us to an island for refugees. We walk off the ship on a wooden plank, away from the ocean, toward land. Most of the island is covered in rocks and trees. Here we are, the two of us, Giang and I, on this very special day, this very great day. It feels wonderful to be off of the ocean, off of the cramped fishing boat, and off of the rescue ship. It feels even better to be able to walk on land. Because we have not walked on solid ground for so long, my legs are as stiff as bamboo shoots. But I don't care. For the very first time in five days, my brother and I know there's a good chance we will live to see many more days.

So much has happened in a short amount of time. I think back. For most of my life, every day was the same, nothing was different. Then, without warning, everything changed. Since leaving South Vietnam, nothing is the same as it was. We left behind all things familiar. We left our home. We left our family. We left our church and our school. We left behind the only life we knew.

We were afraid we might die in the middle of the ocean with eighteen strangers, never to see our family again. If we had died going down to the bottom of this big, blue sea, our father and mother would always wonder about us. They would never know what became of their two sons. I want mother and father to know we made it. I want them to know our story. Someday I hope to tell them how much I missed them and how much I still love them.

There are officials here, on this island. They talk to us. They tell us where to go and what to do. I see rows of what they call "boat people." Most are adults. Some adults have children with them. I don't see many children like us, alone, with no adults. The two of us must stick together. I will not leave Giang's side. I cannot lose sight of my older brother among all these strangers with unfamiliar faces. I do not want to be separated from him because he is all I have.

The officials tell us this island is off the coast of Thailand, but they don't know how long we will be here, sleeping on the ground, in tents. They can't tell us what the future will bring, or where we might go next. All I know is, I'm glad to be on land. I'm relieved to no longer be surrounded by salty, blue water, and I am thankful to be alive. At least I'm not alone. I have my big brother. We have each other. *Thank you, God!*

CHAPTER 7

*The Lord himself goes before you
and will be with you; he will never
leave you nor forsake you. Do not
be afraid; do not be discouraged.*
— Deuteronomy 31: 8

After a few months, Giang and I, along with
many others, are told to climb onto trucks and into
buses because we are moving to a larger refugee camp.
This new place, Camp Song La does not seem much
better or much worse than where we were before. At
first, everything looks about the same. Just like before,
we're surrounded by a tall fence. We're kept inside this
fence and cannot come or go at will. We can only stay
and move around inside the boundary.

At this camp, we sleep inside a long, wooden building
on separate wooden beds, each with its own thin mat-
tress, pillow, and cover. The beds are arranged in rows

along both sides of the building, with a space to walk down the middle. There are many buildings with many beds. Each bed is separated by a curtain. It is not comfortable, but Giang and I both agree we sleep much better here than we did on the boat or inside the tent.

We sleep in the same clothes we wear all day, every day. If we need to relieve our bowels or bladder in the middle of the night, we must go outside. This doesn't bother either of us because we're used to it. Our house in South Vietnam didn't have an indoor toilet.

Mealtime is an important part of the daily routine. Twice a day, when a bell rings, people form lines. Each person is given a small bowl of uncooked rice and a small strip of uncooked meat. We are told it is pork. Everyone must cook their own meat over an open fire. Sometimes we need help with this. There's water or a special kind of milk to drink.

After a few months, we move again. We are now at Camp Sieu Kieu. Not everything at this camp is the same as before. Here, something very important and unexpected happens. As Giang and I wait to get our morning's food ration, we recognize a familiar face, the face of our uncle. We can't believe our good fortune! This uncle, our mother's brother, is here with his three boys, our cousins. We are all very excited to be reunited. Like us, they escaped from South Vietnam on a small boat. While we sit on the ground, eating our food, we share stories. I am happy to be with family.

Because my brother and I are both minors, with no parents, the officials allow us to stay with our uncle. This is especially good, because once again, after a few months, we are sent to another camp. This time, when we arrive at Camp Bananicom, Giang and I are not alone. We are with relatives. Among the many faces, the six of us are once again happy and surprised to see another family member, a distant uncle, also a refugee from South Vietnam.

At this camp, we are given everything we need to write to our parents, but I must not lie, Giang does most of the writing. Sometimes, I write a few words or draw simple pictures. In our first letter, we tell our mother and father where we are, how much we miss them, and that we are with our two uncles and three cousins. We give our letter to the officials to send. It is a relief to be able to write to our parents, telling them we are safe, but it would be even better if we could tell them this in person.

I am certain my parents will find comfort and happiness in knowing Giang and I are no longer by ourselves. We're part of a family of seven. All of us stick together, and all of us spend time in the camp's school, learning to read, write, and speak English. There is not much else to do here, which makes each day seem long.

Since time here passes slowly, I have many opportunities to think about the past. I think often of my family, but the pictures in my head are not as bright and perfect as they were. These once clear images are beginning to fade, and this bothers me. It makes me sad. It makes me worried.

My mother's gentle smile and my father's strong hands are getting harder for me to imagine in my mind. I have trouble hearing their voices in my head. I don't ever want to forget about them, and I don't want them to ever forget about me. I must hang onto my memories. It is important to remember everything.

The seven members of our small family group stay at Camp Bananicom for over two years. No one is sad when we are given the news we are going to America. Mostly we are relieved and excited. After living in refugee camps for so many days and nights, it will feel good to live someplace else. I admit, I am a little scared, knowing my life will soon change. Sometimes change is a good thing, but not always. We will see.

PART 2

INTO
THE DARKNESS

CHAPTER 8

Not only so, but we also rejoice in our sufferings, because we know that suffering produces perseverance; perseverance, character; and character, hope. — Romans 5: 3

It is November of 1985 when my brother, two uncles, three cousins and I leave the refugee camp in Thailand and fly into the San Francisco airport. We are told a church in Oakland, California is sponsoring us. Some people meet us at the airport and take us to a tiny, two bedroom apartment in Oakland. Here, we are reunited with another, older cousin that came to America before us. Now we are a family of eight males. I am the youngest, so I am the last one to choose on which part of the floor I will sleep.

I go with Giang and my cousins to school. It is decided I will start out in third grade. Most of the students in my class are taller and bigger. My mother told me when I was born in 1977, I was born too soon, before I had time to grow into a full sized baby inside her belly. The doctors wanted her to have an abortion, but she refused. When I was born, I was small, weighing only two pounds, two ounces. I'm still small and skinny for my age. Maybe this will always be so. I do not know.

Growing up, I had difficulty talking. I often stuttered. Now, I must speak in a whole different way, in an unfamiliar language. Most of the time I speak Vietnamese, but when I'm not around people from my home country, I try to say English words. I don't always speak these words correctly. I think, because of my small size and the way I talk, I'm picked on at school.

Also, because I don't have nice clothes, I'm bullied in our neighborhood. I often wear the same red jacket. At first it had white sleeves, but now they have turned a dirty brown. My socks are so filthy and soiled, when I take them off at night they do not bend. They stand up straight on the floor.

There's a big boy in our neighborhood that I do not like. Omar is mean to everyone. He bit my brother, Giang, on the ear. His bite left lasting red teeth marks. He punched me in the face and threatened me with a knife, pointing it at my throat. He beat up my cousin. On Halloween, he pushed me down, beat me up, and stole my bag of candy. I try to stay away from him, but that is not always possible. I get tired of being picked on. I get tired of being bullied. To me this is a big problem. I hope this problem gets better soon.

I am beginning to understand my days here in America are going to be very different from my days in South Vietnam. They are also very different from my days at the refugee camps in Thailand. My problems here are not the same as they were when I was in those places. Many things have changed. We are all trying to get by, trying our best to fit in. There are eight of us living together, yet I feel so alone. I miss my father very much! I wish he could be here too.

My uncle, my mother's brother, tries to be like a father, but this is not an easy task. He faces many challenges. After buying food and paying the monthly rent, there is no money left over for any of us to have new clothes or new shoes. There is no money to spend on anything extra. My uncle is given money to take care of my brother and me, but with so many people to support, whatever money he has does not last long. It does not go far.

I do not get my hair cut often. I almost never go to the barber shop, because going there costs money. It is difficult to ask my uncle for cash. I have found it is easier to let my hair grow. My hair is straight and long, past my shoulders.

When our class goes on field trips, I must ask my uncle for money to pay the fees. I must also ask him for money to pay for my lunch. I don't like to ask him for anything, especially money, so I don't go along when my class takes trips. It is easier just to stay home.

I've been thinking, I need money of my own. If I had money, that would solve some of my problems. Having money will make my life better, it will make my life easier. It would be a relief if I never again had to ask my uncle to pay for the things I want or need. With my own money, I can reach into my pocket for the cash. I must find a way to get dollar bills into my hands and into my pockets. Now, all I have to do is figure out how to make this happen.

CHAPTER 9

Be careful, or your hearts will be weighed down with dissipation, drunkenness and the anxieties of life, and that day will close on you unexpectedly like a trap. — Luke 21: 34

The eight of us move often. For a short time, we live with my uncle's friend and her family. When she drives in her car with her kids, she takes me along. She says, since I'm in fourth grade, I'm old enough to stay in the car and watch them while she runs errands. Sometimes, she gives me a candy bar for helping, so I do as she says.

On this particular day, it's raining. My uncle's friend is in a hurry and doesn't see the stop sign. The car we are in gets slammed on the side by an oncoming vehicle. Everyone in our car screams. As the car spins, we spin. The back right window next to me shatters, and a big chunk of glass sticks into my face, slicing me under my right cheek bone.

With lights flashing and sirens blaring, I'm rushed in an ambulance to a nearby hospital. Doctors remove the glass and poke me with needles. I get many stitches to close the wound, starting beside my nose and running in a curved line, under my cheek.

A nurse, sitting beside me on my bed, hands me a mirror. She tells me I might have a big scar, about two inches long. I stare at my reflection. She says, "Vu, don't worry. Your scar will not look so bad. You're a boy. It will make you look tough." Right now it hurts too much to smile, but I think she is right.

After a little while, our small family group once again moves. Leaving my uncle's friend's home, we transfer our few belongings into another apartment. It seems to me we never stay in any one place for very long. Since money is scarce, the apartments we rent are always small, always dark, and always dingy.

There's very little space for my cousins and me to do much of anything inside. When my uncles are home, our indoor activities are limited to staring at the walls or staring at the small television set. When my uncles are gone, we choose a different activity. We fight. My uncles are gone a lot, so we fight a lot.

My uncles get frustrated and upset over all the fighting that goes on in our apartments. Since I'm the youngest and smallest, and since there are four of them and only one of me, I'm the one they pick on. My brother, Giang, isn't around to help protect me. He is always with his friends, which means I am on my own.

In the very last hour of my final day in fifth grade, I get kicked out of school for fighting. I'm told by the adults in charge, I am not allowed to come back. They tell my uncle he must find a new school for me in the fall. This does not make my uncle happy, but it does not bother me, because I hate school.

School is not where I belong. Like Giang, I begin spending less time at home and more time with other Vietnamese boys in the neighborhood. We hang out on the street corners and around coffee shops. This beats being at home, and it is definitely better than being in school.

The streets are where I belong, where I fit in. Now is the right time for me to become part of a gang called the V Boyz. The V stands for Vietnamese. I'm proud to be part of their group. My problem of being picked on and bullied has been solved, because when I'm with them they protect me. We stick together. They are more than friends-they are like brothers; they are my family. Being one of the V Boyz gives me an identity.

As gang members we are active at night. When the sun goes down, we come out. We stand around smoking cigarettes and weed. We drink liquor and forty-ounce bottles of Old English beer. Not only do we smoke weed, we smoke crack and snort cocaine.

I have no worries because the older gang members get us younger gang members anything we want. They get us what we need. I'm one of the youngest members of the gang, and I might be one of the smallest members too, but my size and age does not matter to them. Out on the streets, with the V Boyz, is where I am supposed to be. My mind is made up. I want to be just like them.

The older gang members become my new teachers. They work with me to give me the skills I must have to survive on the streets. They teach me how to buy and sell drugs. From them I learn how to steal cars. I learn how to steal car parts. They show me how to break into houses. They show me how to use all the different kinds of guns. These older gang members are very good teachers. Because of them spending time with me, showing me how things are done, I have become a very good student. This is the right kind of school for me.

No longer do I need to ask my uncle or anyone else for cash. With my new skills, I now have ways of getting my own money. It feels good to have dollar bills in my hands and in my pockets! Another problem has been solved.

CHAPTER 10

Do not set foot on the path of the wicked or walk in the way of evil men. Avoid it, do not travel on it; turn from it and go on your way. — Proverbs 4: 14 - 15

Since I was kicked out of my old school, I must begin my sixth grade year at an entirely different one. Changing schools has not changed my attitude, so I don't do well here either. I don't like anything about school, and I don't fit in. Most of the time I just skip going altogether. Nobody seems to care if I show up for class or not.

A big part of my day and night is spent hanging out, on the streets with the V Boyz. This is where I want to be. When I am with them, I feel like I'm important, like I am somebody. When I am with them, I know they will always watch out for me. They will always have my back.

Even though I don't like school, what I like even less is to be home, in the apartment with my two uncles. When I don't listen, or when I talk back, they hit me and knock me around to make me mind, so I stay away from them as much as possible. Besides, they have their own problems, and they don't need me, bothering them.

To avoid being home, I find plenty of other places to sleep at night other than our cramped, crowded apartment. Many nights I sleep outside on the sidewalk or on the front porch steps. Some nights, if it's raining, I'll sleep inside a van or car. Other nights I crawl through my friend's open basement window and sleep there, curled up on the damp, dirty, cement floor.

My mind tells me there must be a better place on this earth than here, with my uncles and cousins, so I run away. My friend Bao and I start out for Los Angeles. Bao is also a member of the V Boyz. He's old enough to drive so we head out together.

When we get to Los Angeles we search for and find another Vietnamese gang. This gang is called Da V. It's bigger and more powerful than our gang back in Oakland. Two main gang bosses own several houses in the city where their members can hang out, drink, party, and conduct business.

Thirty year old Anh Minh Den, also known as Big Homie, is the main boss. Hung Meo is second in command. Together they oversee drug deals and robberies. Together they make sure their profits keep coming in. Since I'm young, with very little street experience, Big Homie takes me under his wing. He teaches me where to go and how to operate as a drug dealer. He gives me confidence. I look up to both of them.

If it's a night when we're not working, then we party. At these parties we do drugs, drink alcohol, and play around with girls and guns. Our parties are always loud and noisy. During one of these parties, my friends and I sit in a circle on the floor. Bao jokingly picks up a nearby handgun, pointing it directly at my chest. Speaking Vietnamese, someone tells him, "Hey man, quit fooling around with that gun. Put it down!"

Bao lowers the gun with the barrel pointing down. As he does this, it accidentally goes off, blowing a gaping hole in the floor. I'm visibly shaken. Silence fills the room. All eyes are on Bao and me. First, I look at the hole in the floor. Then looking over at Bao I say to him, "Are you kidding me? What were you thinking? You could have killed me!" Bao just shrugs. In a matter of seconds, all is forgotten, and the party continues, late into the night.

There are complaints in the neighborhood about gang activities in one of the houses. My guess is that maybe the cops have been watching, secretly observing what goes on, because one night they conduct a surprise raid. Nobody knows it is coming. When it is over, everyone inside is hauled off to jail. Everything in the house is taken as evidence. I go to jail for weeks, then I'm moved to a group home for boys under the age of eighteen. It is run by an older couple.

After a few days, I'm given a ticket and escorted to the bus station. I keep looking over my shoulder for my chance to escape, but there's always someone beside me or in back of me, hovering, watching, checking. Consequently, I do the only thing left for me to do. I climb on board the bus while handing the driver my ticket. Whether I like it or not, I'm going back to Oakland.

When I return to Oakland, it isn't long before I get picked up for burglary. This time, since I am under eighteen, I'm sent to Juvenile Hall. After being there for months, I decide I've had enough of this rotten place. I want out, I need out, so I plan my escape.

On most days, the routine at this detention center is the same. In the afternoon, the boys are allowed to go outside for a break. The facility is on a hill, but fortunately for me it has no fences. There are only a few guards and wardens patrolling the area, which also works to my advantage.

I contact my friend, Bao, and tell him to be ready to meet me on a nearby road with his car. I give him the exact time and date for my planned escape. When the day arrives, Bao drives his car up to the designated spot. I'm unable to see if he's there, but trusting him, I run as fast as I can, pumping my arms and legs with all of my might, never looking back.

Gasping for breath, and weak from sprinting so fast, I'm happy to see Bao waiting in his car with the motor running. I dive through the open door and yank it closed. Bao steps on the gas and speeds away, turning many corners, attempting to throw any would-be followers off our trail.

When we get far enough away, onto the freeway, Bao and I look at each other. Full of relief, we at first smile, then we begin to laugh out loud. I can hardly believe it. My wild plan worked! We outsmarted them! I am free!

CHAPTER 11

Wisdom is better than weapons of war,
but one sinner destroys much good.
— Ecclesiastes 9: 18

Over the next few years, I return to Los Angeles

many times. Whenever I arrive, Big Homie sets me up with a good supply of guns for free. He says he is always glad to help out a friend. I take these supplies back to Oakland, to the V Boyz. They are happy to have the weapons.

I only stop seeing my mentor, Big Homie, when I hear he is caught in a hit. He, his girlfriend, a waitress, and one other person are shot and killed inside the International Cafe coffee shop. Through the grapevine, I also hear his second in command, Hung Meo, was kidnapped and chopped up into pieces. Somebody really wanted them dead. I am disturbed and shaken by this terrible news. I am also saddened because I looked up to them, and now they are both gone. I will always miss them. They were good to me.

From the two of them, as well as from other, older gang members I have learned so much. I have learned many gang members have guns, sometimes multiple guns and multiple types of guns. When driving around, we must keep these guns hidden in our car's glove compartment, underneath the car's hood, or somewhere on us, covered by our clothes. That way, when we get pulled over by a cop, the guns aren't in plain sight. When I'm carrying a gun, I feel it proves to the world I am tough. When I possess such a powerful weapon, I am convinced nobody dares to mess with me.

At a young age, I learned one of the quickest ways to get cash is to use a screwdriver to break into a car and steal its radio. Of course, gang leaders always demand their share of the profits. Sometimes they will get an order for a particular car. Then we are told to take the whole car, not just the radio or its parts. They especially like us to steal the more expensive cars. These they sometimes ship overseas. They'll tell us what they want, then three or more of us work together to make it happen.

With practice, we become good at what we do. Everyone's satisfied when all goes right, and we come back with a car. Unfortunately, there are times when things don't go as planned. At a young age I learned, when something goes wrong, someone always pays the price.

Late one night, three of us V Boyz go to East 27th Street to steal a car. Duc, Hien and I find the one we want, parked along the road, away from street lights. Duc, the driver, pulls up close, a couple of feet behind the vehicle we want to steal. We're about to make our move when someone from the neighborhood turns onto the street, into a nearby driveway. This person sees us and guesses what we are planning to do. We hear a loud, angry voice yell, "Hey! Stop!"

Duc and I immediately turn and run away, but Hien, staying in the back of our parked car, doesn't run with us. Thinking the neighbor can't possibly know he's there, he crouches down and doesn't move. The only thing Hien can do now is remain hidden, in the back of the car. Here, he waits for our return, waits for us to come and rescue him.

A few blocks away, in the shadowy darkness, Duc and I plot what to do next. Only when we think it is safe to return, will we make our move. Much time passes. Under cover of a night sky, the two of us sneak back to our car. Here our friend, Hien, has been patiently waiting, slouched down, out of sight in the rear seat.

Duc carefully opens the door and slips onto the front seat, behind the wheel. Keeping low, I quietly go to the opposite side of the car. I open the door and sit on the passenger side of the front seat. We don't see any sign of the angry neighbor. We are certain this person believes the excitement is over for the night and has gone to bed.

After Duc turns the key and starts the engine, we discover just how wrong we were. The neighbor has not gone to bed! Like our friend, he too has been waiting for our return. Also like our friend, he too has been hiding.

All along, this person has been crouched behind a car, waiting in the shadows, with a gun pointing in our direction. Duc catches a glimpse of the weapon in the moonlight. Stepping on the gas, he turns sharply. Our tires squeal. We hear many bullets hit the metal of our car in rapid succession. Most seem to be aimed at the car's back, left side. As we get farther away, the bullets stop coming.

After driving a few blocks, Duc pulls the car over to the side of the road. The two of us, sitting in the front, look at each other and breathe a sigh of relief.

Everything seems to have worked out in the end. There will be another chance for us to steal a car, but at least we successfully rescued our friend and made our escape without getting caught...or so we thought.

CHAPTER 12

Why, you do not even know what will happen tomorrow. What is your life? You are a mist that appears for a little while and then vanishes. — James 4: 14

Before we can congratulate each other on our successful get-a-way, Duc and I hear a raspy voice behind us, coming from the back seat. It's the voice of Hien. He says, "I'm hit." Hearing these two words makes a chill run through my body. Immediately, Duc glances up into his rear view mirror. I twist around. Looking back, I see Hien sitting and leaning against the seat, as if nothing unusual happened. His eyes are open, but his face looks pale and expressionless. I stare at him. No words are spoken. I reach back, across the seat to grasp and raise his left arm. It is limp. There's blood! There's lots of blood! As I let go of his arm, Hien slumps over.

Breaking all speed limits, Duc drives to Highland Hospital. I'm afraid. I'm shaking. I try to reassure my friend by telling him we'll be there soon. Duc slams on the brakes in front of the emergency entrance. I race inside to get someone, anyone, to come to our car. We helplessly watch as strangers dressed in white carefully lift Hien from the back seat onto a stretcher with wheels.

Duc and I tell our friend in Vietnamese we will see him tomorrow. I say to him, "Hang in there, man." We know he is strong. We reassure ourselves by telling one another that he'll be up and around by morning. Then we stand close by, watching as doctors with many instruments rush our friend, through a door and down a hallway. There's nothing we can say or do to change what happened. It's too late for that.

The two of us ride in a police car to the station. By now it is the middle of the night. They make us sit on chairs. They ask us many questions. We tell them what we know, leaving out the part about our attempted car theft. We tell them our story so it sounds like another random shooting in the hood.

By morning we are free to go. Before we leave, an officer pulls us off to the side. In a cold, detached voice, he says the hospital called to say our friend, Hien, died. I feel like I have been punched in the gut. All of a sudden, I'm dizzy.

This cop must be mistaken. This cannot be so. We were just with our friend, our brother, a few hours ago. He was talking to us. Nobody should die from a bullet to the shoulder. I feel so very sad. I also feel angry at the person who did this. I don't know what to say. I don't know what to do. I wish this was all a bad dream, so I could wake up and find Hien still alive.

Duc and I leave the police station in silence. I shake my head in disbelief as I think to myself. *This is NOT how it's supposed to be!* But, I'm learning, this is how it is. This is how it will be from now on.

Hien and I are about the same age. He is my close friend, and now he's gone. I will miss him. Many people attend the funeral. There are many flowers and many more tears. I help carry Hien's casket. I watch knowing, as they lower him into the ground, it could have been me in his place.

My heart aches. I have not talked to my mom or dad in years! I need them right now! I want to cry out, *Mom, Dad, where are you when I need you? My two brothers, my two sisters, where are you guys? Where is my family? I love and miss you all. I need you here, beside me!* I feel so alone!

CHAPTER 13

The Lord will rescue me from every evil attack and will bring me safely to his heavenly kingdom. To him be glory forever and ever. Amen. — 2 Timothy 4: 18

The Da Thao Coffee Shop, on East 12th Street in

Oakland, is one of the places we like to hang out. Drug deals go down here. Most of our "business connections" are made here. We protect the shop from other gangs. In return, the shop's Vietnamese owner, the man we call Anh Dung, which translated means "older brother" gives our gang money each month.

There is kind of a rule every gang member lives by. It goes, "If one gang member has a problem, we all have a problem." Like I said before, we are friends, but we're more than that, we're brothers. One morning Bao comes to us saying he has a problem with a gang from San Jose, which is about thirty minutes away. He doesn't give us any specific information about this problem, and no one asks. The reason is not important. We often say, "We always down for the Homies," meaning, "We're always there for each other."

Bao says this San Jose gang wants to talk. They want to meet the V Boyz at the Da Thao Coffee Shop. We agree to the meeting, but we don't trust this gang from San Jose, so we begin to prepare. We want to be ready for the unexpected.

All gang members arm themselves. We each hide guns in the back of our pants. The gun's handle is hidden by our shirt. Then we stash guns in different locations throughout the coffee shop. We hide oozies, AK 47's and 9 millimeter handguns behind the shop's counter, nearby on a shelf, beneath tables and in the back storage area. We also place guns around and underneath bushes outside. Loaded guns are all over, ready if we need them...just in case.

The day to talk arrives. It is time. Some of the V Boyz sit inside. There are customers ordering and eating food at the tables, unaware there's a planned meeting between two gangs at this location. I'm standing out-side, in front of the coffee shop, off to one side of the building. Bao is inside, waiting. Everyone who knows about the meeting is tense, anticipating what will happen next.

I see two red, two-door Acura Legends pull up in front of the coffee shop. There are several guys in each car. The windows go down and someone leans out calling, "Hey, Bao, come out here. Let's talk." There is only silence. Then all hell breaks loose!

Without warning, like a scene from a gangster movie, a sudden flurry of bullets explodes into the coffee shop. The sound of bullets hitting the building and breaking the glass is deafening. This surprise attack lasts for forty-five seconds to one minute, but it seems like it lasts forever. Then, as suddenly as it started, the bullets stop, and the two red cars speed away.

There's much screaming and crying. Bright, flashing lights and ear-piercing sirens fill the air. Dozens of police and rescue vehicles line the streets. The entire area is blocked off with crime scene tape. Many people are hurt. It's a miracle no one is dead.

After all of that planning and preparation, we didn't have a chance to shoot back. The attack was so sudden and fierce, everyone was caught by surprise. When it began raining bullets, I was in shock, I froze. I didn't know what to do!

Thank You God. Thank You Jesus.

The Vietnamese Gang Task Force, an extended arm of the police, makes me sit in their car while they ask me questions. They don't keep me long after I tell them I was an innocent customer, a bystander who just happened to be in the area.

When I get out of the cop car, I don't leave the area. Instead, I watch silently as the wounded are put on stretchers and removed from inside the building. On this day, I feel lucky. Unlike many of my friends and fellow gang members, I will not be riding in an ambulance to a nearby hospital to have bullets removed from my body.

CHAPTER 14

The one who sows to please his sinful nature, from that nature will reap destruction; the one who sows to please the spirit from the Spirit will reap eternal life. — Galatians 6: 8

In and around Oakland and the San Francisco

Bay area, gang wars are a common part of life. Maybe that's because there are so many different gangs. There's a gang for every race and nationality. Besides the Vietnamese gangs, there are the Bloods, the Crips, White Power gangs, Black gangs, Mexican gangs, Asian gangs, Samoan gangs, and Chinese gangs. Gang wars start for a variety of reasons. Over the years, I've learned a gang war can start by simply giving someone the wrong kind of "look."

If that certain "look" is given, the questions, "What's up? What you lookin' at?" almost always come next. If I am with the V Boyz, and an outsider looks at any one of us in a way we don't like, I can almost guarantee a fight will follow. Of course, I could be mistaken, but I think this is what might have happened to My, the fellow V Boyz gang member.

I've been in jail many times, but not nearly as many as My. During his latest term behind bars, he made good use of his jail time. He worked out a lot and left the place looking buff. He's in perfect shape, so what does he do? He goes around, letting people see his new abs, his new sculpted physique.

Not long after he's been out and about, he comes back to the V Boyz with a problem. Like I said before, we don't ask, and the reason for the problem is not important, but that doesn't stop me from making a guess. This time, my hunch is his problem has something to do with his giving or receiving the wrong kind of "look." Whatever the reason, My is badly beaten. The Chinese gang from across the bridge in San Francisco uses heavy, metal chains and thick 4 x 4 boards on him.

When he comes to us with his problem, he's in bad shape. His face looks pretty messed up. After I see what they did to our friend, our brother, and fellow gang member, I immediately want revenge. I grab my shotgun and organize a group to start driving around, looking for the guys who are responsible for this beating. We drive all over with no sign of the Chinese gang, so we head back home to Mong Mo, another of the V Boyz coffee shop hangouts.

Well, surprise, surprise! There they are. Some members of the Chinese gang are standing outside, just waiting for us to show up. With their chains and 4 x 4 sticks, they're gathered around their Toyota Celica two-door, across from the coffee shop, ready for a fight. When they see us, they hold up their weapons, threatening to use them.

Uncontrolled rage flares inside of me. I spring from the car, running across the street toward them, firing my shotgun. Not wanting to get hit, the Chinese gang members see me and scatter in all directions. One of them runs to a nearby Shell Gas Station.

Two of us see him and follow close behind. He bursts through the door of the station and jumps over the counter, screaming at the cashier to call the cops. We leave before the cops arrive. It's over for now, but tensions between the gangs remain.

Tired and fed up with the ongoing fighting between the Oakland Vietnamese gang and the San Francisco Chinese gang, a man known to everyone as O.G. calls a meeting. The letters O.G. stand for the first letters in the words Original Gangster, but he is also called Anh Hoang.

He's in his thirties and has the respect of both sides because he has paid his dues. It's a fact, any gang member in his thirties has beaten the odds. By that age, most are either in prison or in a casket buried six feet underground. O.G. gets both sides to sit, talk, and work things out, but how long this gang truce will last, no one knows. I'm betting it won't last long.

No matter how hard I try to ignore it, a voice in my head keeps asking, *Is this how you want to live the rest of your life?* When things calm down, I have time to think. I think about how lucky I am nobody was seriously injured or killed when I was full of rage, firing my shotgun at the other gang. If that had happened, I'd be in prison right now. I don't want to end up, living my life in a cell behind bars, with nothing to look at besides four bare walls, a bed, a sink, and a toilet.

So, here I am, Lord. My name is Vu Pham, and I have a problem. I'm not going to my gang about this problem, instead I am coming to you, Lord. My problem is, I don't know how to change. I see no way out, so I really could use your help. Please, Lord, I'm asking you, I'm begging you, to light my way.

PART 3

INTO THE LIGHT

CHAPTER 15

*Though I walk in the midst of trouble,
you preserve my life; you stretch out
your hand against the anger of my
foes, with your right hand you save me.*
— Psalms 138: 7

Because I'm in a gang, I am always on the move.

It's not good for a gang member to stay in one place for
too long. By moving around, it becomes harder for the
cops and my parole officer to catch me. If I am picked
up for any reason, they only need to look on the computer and read my file. Then they haul me back to jail
or Juvenile Hall. So, I keep moving.

Even though I never stay in one place for long, I'm
still connected to my gang. Staying connected makes
me money. It helps me decide where I should go next
to do business. It is through one of these connections
in San Francisco that I meet Mylinh. She is a Chinese/

Vietnamese/American. She's more than a beautiful girl. She is smart, kind, and she helps change my life.

We are introduced through a friend of a friend in a San Francisco gang. I think it might be fate or the hand of God guiding me. When we first meet, I had just gotten out of jail for burglary. Mylinh's boyfriend had just been handed a long term prison sentence. I think it is meant to be, that we become friends, that we become a couple.

The two of us have much in common. We spend many hours of each day hanging out with gangs. Neither of us like school. She drops out after finishing eighth grade. I begin my freshman year of high school at Oakland Tech, four years in a row. Both of us like to party. We play cards, smoke, drink, eat at restaurants, and drink coffee at the various gang coffee shops.

For a short time, I leave Mylinh to visit two friends in Durham, North Carolina. When they lived in Oakland, these guys, named Truong and GI Joe, were members of the V Boyz. Now they work for a Vietnamese company in Durham.

It feels good to see them, to talk about old times, to smoke weed, and get drunk together. It feels good to just hang out. At some point, we become tired of sitting around. We hop in GI Joe's black Mercedes and go to "the projects," looking to see what drugs we can buy. Truong, better known as Fat Boy, sits in the front with GI Joe the driver, which means I sit in the back. It's a nice night, so all of our car windows are down.

As we're cruising around, Fat Boy sees someone, a man who reminds him of a TV personality, standing on the street corner near our car. When GI Joe stops at the stop sign, a very drunk Fat Boy leans out of the window and calls, "Hey man, you look just like Montel Williams!"

This apparently was the wrong thing to say. To teach us a lesson, the guy pulls out a revolver. Thinking I was the cocky one who yelled at him, he points the gun at me. The gun's barrel is aimed directly at my head, with his finger poised on the trigger. Then, everything seems to happen in slow motion.

There's an instant when our eyes meet. We see each other. It's as if he's looking into my soul. Thinking, deciding, he tilts his head while he hesitates. I don't know why, but he doesn't shoot, he doesn't pull the trigger. My mind races. I have a strange feeling this has happened before.

Then I remember! Images of when I was a kid on a fishing boat flash before me. I picture the pirate giving me that exact look, that same soul penetrating look I

71

see in this man's eyes. How can this be? How can the same thing happen twice? Both times, I could have been shot, I could have been killed.

Catching a glimpse of the gun, GI Joe steps on the gas. Now the man with the revolver starts shooting. A bullet flies through the opening of the right front window, striking Fat Boy in the shoulder. It happened again! For the second time tonight, I'm reminded of an incident from my past. I'm reminded of the time my friend, Hien, was shot in the shoulder. On the night he was shot, he was sitting in the back seat, where I'm sitting now. But there is a difference-I am fine.

GI Joe speeds to the nearest hospital emergency room. We help our friend inside, and the three of us are guided into a small room. Fat Boy rests on a bed. The doctor looks at his wound and says something our friend does not expect to hear. "Well, the bullet landed in a good location. It shouldn't give you any long term trouble where it's at. I'm not going to remove it. We'll disinfect it, stitch you up where the bullet entered, and you're free to go home." I am relieved my friend will be OK, but I wish Hien could have had the same results.

Soon after that shooting incident, I return to Oakland, to the V Boyz, and to Mylinh. For many days, my visit to North Carolina continues to haunt me. What stopped the man on the street corner from shooting me? What stopped the pirate from pulling the trigger so many years ago?

There were many times in my life I could have been killed, but I was not. Is there a reason for this? I have a nagging feeling someone is watching over me, protecting me. Is it God? These questions keep popping back into my head. I don't have answers to my questions. I only know, I can't continue to live like this. I keep thinking something in my life has got to change. I silently pray, *Please Lord, I can't do this on my own. I need your help.*

CHAPTER 16

Your own conduct and actions have brought this upon you. How bitter it is! How it pierces to the heart.
— Jeremiah 4: 18

It's been some time since I've seen my brother, Giang. I am happy he has returned home, to Oakland. While gone, he was in and out trouble with the law many times. He tells me he's been trying to straighten out his life. He has a job, he's going to counseling sessions and taking classes at a junior college. It's good to have him back. I've missed my brother.

Giang has not been back long when our cousin, Thuc, rushes into Bao's house. He finds my brother hanging out with two friends who came with him from Los Angeles. Thuc sounds desperate. He needs the three of them to help him with a problem.

He says he needs them to come with him. There's a gang called Wah Ching, waiting for him a few blocks away, in front of the Mong Mo Coffee Shop. Giang and his two friends don't ask questions. Thuc has a problem, and that's all they need to know. The four of them grab their guns and hop into the Thunderbird parked in Bao's driveway.

As they approach the coffee shop, they realize they are outnumbered. There are between ten and fifteen members of the Wah Ching gang standing outside, armed and ready. Giang, Thuc, and the other two move quickly. Using the element of surprise, Giang slams on the brakes, and they scramble out. Not one word is spoken, but both sides immediately start shooting. Many bullets pass between the two groups.

There are injuries. Much worse than the injuries, it appears someone in the Wah Ching gang may have been killed. Thuc is bleeding, he's been shot in the leg. The four of them know they need to get away. Giang and his friends help Thuc escape on foot. They return the short distance to Bao's house.

After Giang gets his cousin safely into the house, he and his friends disappear. With a bullet in his leg, Thuc hides inside and calls our uncle. Answering the phone, our uncle hears Thuc's story. A short time later, he parks his car in Bao's drive, trying to do whatever he can to help his nephew out of a bad situation.

Their plans to dodge the cops fail. Thuc and his uncle are captured and taken to the police station. At some point, Thuc tells the cops all he knows. In other words, he squeals on my brother, Giang, and his friends. Having played no part in the gun battle, my uncle is free to go. My cousin, on the other hand, goes to trial for murder.

For a couple of years, Giang and his two friends are able to avoid getting caught. After leaving Bao's the day of the shooting, they make their way to Los Angeles where they join up with the Da V gang. As gang members, their lives do not change. They continue with their criminal lifestyle.

Their luck runs out when they are caught, handcuffed, and arrested for robbery. Unfortunately for them, the computer shows there is much more to their background history than robbery. It lists all of their past offenses. The three of them are individually tried as accessories to murder.

Because Thuc helped the police by snitching on my brother and my brother's friends, he serves the lightest sentence. He goes to prison for ten years. Of the two friends, one serves twenty years, while the other serves twenty-five. My brother is sentenced to "15 years to life." At the time, Giang thinks fifteen years is not so bad, but as it ends up, this is the harshest sentence. The four letter word "life" behind any number makes a big difference. It means Giang could be an old man before he gets out. It means he must, at all times, be a model prisoner or they'll keep him behind bars indefinitely. Maybe he'll be there for the rest of his life. I sincerely hope not.

CHAPTER 17

So don't be afraid; you are worth more
than many sparrows. — Matthew 10: 31

When I think about what happened, I have so
many emotions bottled up inside. I feel bitterness
toward my cousin for dragging my brother into this,
then snitching on him to lighten his own sentence. At
the same time, I feel angry because this happened to
Giang at a time when he was trying to straighten out
his life. I feel sadness for the person who was killed.
I also feel a sense of loss and regret for Giang and
myself because the life we knew as brothers will never
be the same.

Throughout our lives, Giang and I shared so much;
those early years with our parents in South Vietnam,
the unexpected motorcycle ride, five days drifting aimlessly on the ocean, two years surviving as refugees
in Thailand before coming to a strange new country,

America. Though a lot has changed, there is one thing that will never change. Giang will forever be my big brother. He will always be the one I look up to. Of that, I'm certain.

Giang's first stop among many is the Salinas State Prison in Sacramento. When I visit him, experiences we've shared as brothers once again fill my head, weighing heavy on my heart. I don't know what to say to him. There's nothing I can do to help him. He says he worries about me. He doesn't want me to end up in the same mess he's in.

Back when I dropped out of school, Giang stuck with it, graduating from high school at the top of his class. Even though our paths took different directions, we both got caught up in the gang lifestyle. Each of us has done many bad things. I can't help thinking, if this can happen to Giang, it can also happen to me. This thought makes me afraid of my future. I say a silent prayer for Giang. I say one for myself too.

After that first visit with my brother in prison, my thoughts again turn into questions. I've been close to death many times, why have I been spared? Does God have a purpose for me? Because I've done many bad things, will God even listen to my prayers? Will all of my sins be forgiven? Is it too late for me to change?

I think back to the many times our family walked to church. I remember mother telling me about the statue of Jesus on the cross. I can still hear her saying, "Jesus is God's son who died on the cross, so when we ask for forgiveness for the bad things we've done, God will forgive us." *I worry that God has given up on me. I wonder if he even knows who I am.*

CHAPTER 18

I will instruct you and teach you in the way you should go; I will counsel you and watch over you. — Psalms 32: 8

After visiting my brother in prison, I go back to

Oakland and the V Boyz. When I am here with them, it is easy to push aside thoughts of God and God's Son Jesus dying on the cross for my sins. All those questions about the bad things I've done, those questions that were running through my head, no longer seem important. In fact, they now seem silly and foolish.

As time passes, it also becomes easier to worry less about Giang and his future life behind bars. I try to focus only on the present. I no longer want to think about my future and what will happen to me if I stick with a gang. Besides, I don't know how to change or if I even can change. I'm not sure how to make things any different, so I keep doing what I've been doing for so many years. On the streets, with the V Boyz, is where I belong.

My need for money has not changed; it is always present. I go to a street where a known drug dealer does most of his business. I drive up to the dealer. I tell him I'm here to buy drugs. The dealer gives me what I want. Instead of handing over the cash to pay him, I grab the drugs and speed away. I can hear the many bullets from the drug dealer's gun hitting the car's metal, but they all miss me. A few weeks later a friend, a fellow V Boyz gang member, does the exact same routine. It cost him his life.

In Alameda there's a bowling alley with a parking lot full of cars. I go there often, not to bowl, but to steal radios from the cars parked there. While I'm working, focusing on getting at a particular radio, a man with a shotgun sneaks up and points the gun directly at me. I see his face.

He looks as though he's going to pull the trigger, but for the third time in my life something changes this potential shooter's mind. He hesitates, and I take this chance to run away unharmed. I begin wondering if a guardian angel is watching over me. There is always this feeling I can't seem to shake. It's the feeling I'm meant to do more with my life. Silently I pray, *God, do you have a plan for me?*

As if in answer, I get a phone call. It comes a few months after my first visit with friends, GI Joe and Fat Boy. They want me to come back to Durham. They tell me to leave the life of a gang member behind and come to North Carolina.

They say I can work in the nail salon that employs them. In their sales pitch they add, it will be a good experience. It will get me out of Oakland and away from the gangs, plus it will be a way for me to make money. If I decide to come, I will work, and at the same time I'll complete training with other students at the salon. I think this is God's answer to my prayers.

CHAPTER 19

He will wipe every tear from their eyes. There will be no more death or mourning or crying or pain, for the old order of things has passed away.
— Revelation 21: 4

Never in a million years would I leave Mylinh

behind, so we talk it over and together decide to take the plunge. Without looking back, we change the course of our lives. Our new focus will be to learn a skill so we can make an honest living.

We are broke. Since we have no money, our friend and fellow V Boyz gang member, Bong, helps us out. He makes it possible for us to buy two plane tickets from California to North Carolina. Thanks to the kindness of our friend, we are able to board a plane, saying good-bye to our former way of life.

Mylinh and I arrive in Durham. Soon after we get settled, we begin our many long hours of training. We work for free at this beauty salon for six months. In return, they cover our rent for an apartment, and they give us a small allowance for food.

The nail business takes Mylinh and I to many places. We work at private salons, malls, and shopping centers throughout North Carolina, Indiana, and Ohio. We like what we do. We feel we're good at what we do. We're grateful for this opportunity.

At most jobs, Mylinh and I work together during the day. In the evenings we go home to our rental apartment to make supper. We don't have many possessions, which makes it easy for us to pack up and move. If there is an opening at a better salon or an opportunity to advance at a different location, we take it.

We own very few kitchen utensils, and a can opener is not something we have. When preparing food, Mylinh usually hands the unopened cans to me. I use a knife to pry open the lids. First, I jab the knife into the top of the can. Then I circle the lid with the knife's sharp edge and pull up.

One time, while doing this, the knife slips. Its sharp point stabs me on the bridge of my nose, cutting the skin, leaving a scar. If my head or hand had moved even a fraction of an inch in either direction, I would have stabbed myself in the eye. Mylinh and I decide our next purchase will be a can opener.

CHAPTER 20

For if you forgive men when they sin against you, your heavenly Father will also forgive you. But if you do not forgive men their sins, your Father will not forgive your sins. — Matthew 6: 14-15

There is an opening in a salon in Toledo, Ohio.

We move there. While we work and live in Toledo, we drive an SUV. One night, when we're done for the day, I drop Mylinh off at our apartment. Then I drive a few blocks away to fill the SUV with gas. We have no garage, so returning home, I pull up along a curb. I usually park in the area of Hollywood and Detroit streets, close to where we live.

It's a warm evening, my driver's side window is down. A large man walks up to my car. Bending down, he crosses his arms, resting them on my door. He casually leans in, as if he wants to talk. We are face-to-face.

I smile, thinking he is going to ask me for directions. Before I have time to react, he grabs my forehead with his right hand, violently jerking my head back. His left hand reaches in front of me, sticking the pointed end of a curved, metal blade into my neck.

I feel a sharp, cold knife pressing into my flesh. He says he wants all my money. I reach over and give him my wallet. He grabs it and slowly strolls across the street, as if nothing out of the ordinary happened. With my hand, I check my neck for blood. I'm relieved there is none. From my side view mirror I watch him. I can feel my pulse quicken and my muscles tighten. My first impulse is to back up, step on the gas, and run my car over this guy. I want to flatten him. If I move quickly, I can still get him. I shift my car into reverse, ready to even the score.

Then someone or something tells me to STOP. I calm down. I relax. Surprisingly, I shift the car into drive and pull away from the scene. My reaction is totally different from what I would have done in the past. For many years, my immediate impulse was to seek revenge, to make people pay. Slowly, a little bit at a time, I am learning to pause, to listen to God's voice before doing the first thing that pops into my head.

I am trying to change, believing that If I can forgive others, then maybe God will forgive me. This kind of change does not come easily. This kind of change does not happen overnight. With time, and with God's help, I am learning to follow His plan instead of mine.

CHAPTER 21

My son, preserve sound judgment and discernment, do not let them out of your sight; they will be life for you, an ornament to grace your neck.
— Proverbs 3: 21-22

My oldest sister, Theresa, owns a nail salon in

Napoleon, Ohio. Five years after Giang and I come to America, our parents also help my two sisters, Theresa and Tien, escape from South Vietnam. For some time my frightened sisters hid in caves, waiting until our father could find them passage out of our war-torn country. Instead of going to Thailand like Giang and I, they were taken by boat to Malaysia. From there they came to America, staying with an aunt and uncle. Even though our lives have taken separate paths, we've tried to keep in touch over the years.

After some discussion, Mylinh and I both feel we need to find a more permanent place to live. We need to settle away from big cities, in a smaller town where we can put down roots. My sister, Theresa, lets us know she could use some help in her nail salon in Napoleon. She says we can work for her. We appreciate the offer and decide to take her up on it.

Several months pass, and we hear about a two-story, downtown building for rent in nearby Defiance, Ohio. It was a Chinese restaurant which is now closed. Together we go and look. There's space for an apartment on the second floor. There's room for our nail business on the first floor. It seems like the perfect place.

On March 23, 2000, we open up VIP Nails. The year marks the beginning of a new millennium for everyone in the world, but it marks the beginning of a new life for Mylinh and me. Ashamed of my past, I change my name from Vu to Victor. I know it won't always be easy, but I want to start over. My new life will have God and Jesus at the center.

When this same building, the one we rent goes up for sale, we take out a loan and purchase it. By watching our money and working hard, Mylinh and I are able to branch out. We open a second nail salon in Bryan, Ohio. On one snowy, wintery night while driving home from Bryan, I step too hard on the car's brakes, sending it careening to the left. It plunges onto the embankment of a deep ditch. The car flips over, skidding the icy length of the ditch on its roof.

Seat belted in and sitting upside down, I have no control of my car as it slides toward a large pole. The pole, directly ahead, is getting closer. I silently pray, *Please God, stop this car.* My car is totaled but comes to rest inches away from the pole. I crawl out of the car and climb up the ditch bank without a scratch. I'm able to go home, back to Defiance, back to Mylinh, shaken but unharmed. *Thank you, God!*

CHAPTER 22

And so we know and rely on the love God has for us. God is love. Whoever lives in love lives in God, and God in him. — 1 John 4: 16

The year is 2005. I am twenty-seven and Mylinh is twenty-four. Together for eight years, Mylinh and I both agree it is a good time to get married. Our plans for a large wedding are suddenly and unexpectedly postponed when we learn her father is dying of cancer. We have no doubt what we must do, what we need and want to do.

With heavy hearts, the two of us fly to the west coast. We go to Kaiser Hospital in Hayward, California. Here we meet up with Mylinh's mother and close family members. Mylinh is the first of four children to get married, and our wish now is to have an intimate wedding in the hospital room of Peter Au, her father.

Mylinh wants her father to be present at her wedding. It is important he is with her on this special day.

I wear a suit. Mylinh wears a dress and holds in her hands, a small bouquet of flowers. Together we solemnly stand beside her father's bed, with family gathered around. The lights are dim. The time is 7 o'clock in the evening. The room is quiet, except for the soft swishing sound of the machines, working to keep Mylinh's father alive.

It is a simple ceremony. We say our vows before a priest and those in attendance, promising to, "forever love, honor, and cherish each other." Following the ceremony, I kiss the bride. Then Mylinh bends down, tenderly kissing her father on the cheek. She whispers, "I love you," in his ear. Her father dies peacefully at five o'clock the next morning.

We allow one year to pass before flying back to California for our second wedding. This time we have a traditional Chinese-Buddhist ceremony at the Au family home, held specifically for Mylinh's family and friends in San Francisco. The guests sit. Mylinh and I approach, bow, and offer each of them tea in a gold-rimmed, porcelain cup and saucer. Each guest sips the tea and hands us a wedding gift.

I wear a black suit. The bride looks like a princess in her white gown. After the wedding ceremony, there is a large reception at a restaurant for 450 people. Of those guests, 430 are Mylinh's family and friends. We miss her father and wish he was with us to share this special day.

Six months later, we have wedding number three. This one is for my side of the family. Along with my sister, Theresa, and her three children, Mylinh and I fly to Vietnam. It is a twenty-four hour flight. Then we take an eight-hour car ride to arrive at my small village of Kinh 7b Khu 3 in South Vietnam.

Words cannot describe how very good it feels to be back home with mother, father, and my little brother, Tao, who is now a grown man. It is an emotional reunion. Memories and images of my past fill my mind. There are many hugs. There are many tears of happiness. There's much chatter. Everyone's excited to meet Mylinh, my beautiful bride.

For this wedding, we have a traditional Catholic ceremony in the church where I was baptized. It's the same church I attended with my family so many years ago. I can still picture us walking down the dirt road, twice a day, early in the morning and late in the after-noon, to attend worship services. It's the same church where, as a little boy, I stared at the figure of Jesus nailed to the cross.

A large reception is held outside, in the yard by our house. There are 400 guests, all family and friends on my side. Many people from our village come up and ask, "Vu, do you remember me?" I was only six when I left, but I try my best to recall each face. On this happy occasion, it feels good to be at my childhood home, among family and friends, even if it is for a short time.

CHAPTER 23

For I am convinced that neither death
nor life, neither angels nor demons,
neither the present nor the future, nor
any powers, neither height nor depth,
nor anything else in all creation will
be able to separate us from the love
of God that is in Christ Jesus our Lord.
— Romans 8: 38-39

It is a great day when my mother, My Kieu
comes to America. She had to fill out many forms in
order to get permission to come. My father's request
is denied, but he promises to keep trying.

I've missed my mother. It is so good to have her
here. She approves of our nail business and is proud of
what we have done. We spend many hours talking. We
try to make up for all those lost years. While in America,
Mother visits her two daughters. She goes to California

to see my cousins and uncles. She visits her oldest son, Giang, in prison. She gets to know her grandchildren.

After going back and forth for five years, between her family in South Vietnam and her family here in America, my mother finds out she is seriously ill. Doctors tell her she is dying of liver cancer, with only weeks to live. My father, Minh Pham, immediately fills out emergency forms. This time he is granted clearance to come to America. He needs to be with his wife, to comfort her in her final days. They need to be together.

In July of 2012, just two months after her diagnosis, my mother passes away peacefully at Highland Hospital in California, with her husband and family by her side. Our time together is too short. Five years is not nearly long enough. I love my mother, I will always miss my mother. I am sad about those many years we were apart, but I am grateful to God for the time we could be together.

When my father comes to America to be with my dying mother, he does not come alone. He brings three statues with him on the plane. He brings them with him, all the way from our small village of Kinh 7b Khu 3 in South Vietnam. The largest statue is a three foot image of Jesus on the cross. The second statue is the Virgin Mary. The third statue is Saint Joseph.

After my mother's death, my father and I work together to safely secure and mount all three statues on our living room wall. We spend many hours talking and getting to know each other. It feels good to be with him, to work side-by-side with him, to have him here, in our home. My father is in America for three years before he returns to his village, his family, his friends, and his church in South Vietnam.

I am saddened to learn he too is diagnosed with liver cancer. When word comes of his death, I travel back to my childhood home. His funeral is held in the same church where, as a tiny, premature baby, I was baptized, and where, as a grown man, I was married.

My father's body is cremated. Someday, when my brother, Tao, and his family are permitted to come to America, he will bring my father's ashes with him. Then, according to our parents' wishes, the ashes of my father will be added to those of my mother.

I feel as though, with the continual presence of God and Jesus, my life has come full circle. As a child I stared at the statue of Jesus in front of our church in South Vietnam. Back then I had many questions. My mother did her best to answer them. Thanks to my father, as a grown man I can daily gaze upon the statue of Jesus in our living room. Also, for the past nineteen years I have found comfort in focusing upon the face of God's son, Jesus, in Saint Mary's Catholic Church in Defiance.

Still, I have questions. Perhaps I will always have questions, but along the way I have found some answers. I know God is real. I am living proof, God never gives up on anyone, and He has a plan for each of us. I believe, because of Jesus, my sins are forgiven. I have no doubt, there is power in prayer. While on life's journey I have discovered, the stronger my faith becomes, the easier it is for me to stay away from temptation. Knowing all of this, it is important for me to thank God and Jesus every day for the life I now have.

Mounted on our living room wall are the three statues my father lovingly brought with him those thousands of miles from South Vietnam. Beneath the statues of Jesus, Mary, and Joseph are glass shelves with framed pictures of our deceased relatives. Included among them are photographs of Mylinh's father, my mother, and my uncle. In 2015, my father's picture is added to the collection of relatives we will forever love, honor, and miss. I look at their faces and thank God for allowing these people to be a part of my life.

CHAPTER 24

If they obey and serve Him, they will spend the rest of their days in prosperity and their years in contentment.
— Job 36: 11

Through all of our ups and downs, our nail business continues to grow. Enjoying her work, but needing an additional challenge, Mylinh enrolls in the premed program at Defiance College. For a few years she manages to juggle her obligations at VIP Nails with her studies. She sticks with it and earns a diploma. This is amazing for someone who only completed eighth grade, dropping out of high school at the beginning of her freshman year. I am so proud of her. She is proud of herself.

Also needing a challenge, I sign up for Taekwondo lessons at the academy on Spruce Street in Defiance. This combative sport is much like kick boxing. After training for a couple of years, I enter Mixed Martial Arts or MMA cage fighting competitions. The self-discipline I need to train and compete, makes me realize how much I have abused my body with tobacco, drugs, and alcohol. My goal now is to help others avoid the same self-destructive path I followed.

With God's guidance, Mylinh and I transform the back portion of our nail salon into a spacious gym for youth. In the evenings, we push the nail stations aside so the front part of our business can also be used by area youth. Teenage boys of varying ages and backgrounds come after school and train. In the daytime, we do nails. In the evenings, from seven until nine, on Monday through Friday, boys come to learn MMA fighting for free. Mylinh and I buy a large workout mat and workout equipment. We gratefully accept some equipment donations.

I start a group called the VIP Boyz. This is the name I choose because I want each boy to know he is a VIP or Very Important Person. In the evenings, we concentrate on Mixed Martial Arts, boxing, jujitsu, and weight lifting. It keeps the boys in shape, teaches them self-defense, helps them to gain confidence and develops self-respect. More importantly, it gives them something to do, it keeps them off the streets. With the skills they learn and practice, a small guy is able to defend himself against a much larger opponent.

In 2013, Defiance native Ashley Brandon and her partner, Dennis Hohne, hear about our youth training program through Facebook and by talking to area participants. They film a documentary about our program titled, "Punches and Pedicures." It's selected for viewing at the Dayton Film Festival, the Slamdance Film Festival in Utah, as well as many other film festivals throughout the country.

In 2014, because of my success and help in spreading the MMA program and philosophy, I am honored to be inducted into Indiana's Mixed Martial Arts Hall of Fame. My father, still alive at the time, proudly attends the reception with me.

After a good friend dies from a drug overdose, I print large posters that say, "Jesus saves, Heroin kills." Many of my VIP Boyz carry these posters in the annual Defiance Halloween Parade. I park two cars across the road from our business. They are painted with these same words. I fit the cars with special lights, giving them a colorful glow at night. I want kids to see the cars and read the words. I want kids to know these words are true.

I don't like heights, but three times I've gone sky-diving. My highest jump was from 10,000 feet. Each time I wear a shirt that says, "Jesus saves, Heroin kills." While tied to a cord, I've twice jumped 855 feet from the Stratosphere Hotel in Las Vegas, wearing a shirt that says the same thing. I post my jumps and my message on You Tube and Facebook for kids to see.

In 2019, I turned forty-two years old. Over twenty-five years ago, when I was in a gang and part of the drug culture, the drugs were not as powerful, not as addictive as they are today. Now, they are so strong, so potent, kids become easily hooked. This can happen even on their very first try. In the beginning, dealers give their drugs to early users for free, just to get them started. Once a kid gets hooked, it becomes hard to stop using and abusing. That's how the dealers make their money. Kids need to know this, before it's too late. By telling my story and making kids aware, I'm fulfilling God's purpose for me here on earth. This is my life's mission.

POSTSCRIPT

In the same way, let your light shine before men, that they may see your good deeds and praise your Father in heaven. — Matthew 5: 16

For many years, I was too ashamed of my past

to talk about it, so I kept quiet. I kept my experiences hidden. I was afraid people would hear my words and judge me, but God and the Holy Spirit helped me overcome my shame. I truly believe my story of sin and redemption is meant to be told. Through the grace of God and the forgiveness of Jesus, I've been able to stand in front of people, sharing my story and proclaiming the good news that, God and Jesus never gave up on me! If reading about my life keeps even one person, one teenager from going down a similar path, then I have done the job God intended. Every day I thank God for saving my life. Every day I thank Jesus

Thank You God. Thank You Jesus.

for dying on the cross so my sins are forgiven. I almost lost my life, but not my soul. Amen!

DISCUSSION QUESTIONS

1. How can the Bible verse in Chapter 1 help people who are struggling? How does this verse apply to Vu?

2. In Chapter 2, when Vu was on the motorbike, he turned around to see his father one last time. Why did Vu's father disappear so quickly?

3. Give possible reasons why Vu and Giang's parents did not go with them when they escaped South Vietnam?

4. Three periods in a row indicates the omission of words. At the bottom of page 12, there is one unfinished sentence. What words would you use to finish it?

5. In Chapter 4, why didn't the pirate fire his pistol at Vu? List the possibilities. How does this Bible verse apply?

6. How could Chapter 5's Bible verse help Vu at this point in his life? How does it apply to us?

7. While they were at the refugee camps, do you think Vu and Giang brushed their teeth before going to bed? Explain your answer.

8. Give words describing how Vu's parents must have felt receiving letters from their two sons.

9. Vu weighed 2 pounds, 2 ounces when he was born. Why is this considered small? Do you know your birth weight?

10. What reasons does Vu give for being bullied at home and at school? When Vu is bullied, he suffers mentally and physically. What does the Bible verse in Chapter 8 say about suffering?

11. What would you do if you felt like you needed money? Could any of these same ideas have worked for Vu? Explain why or why not.

12. Why do you think Vu finds alternative places to sleep at night in Chapter 10?

13. In Chapter 11, Vu observes, "When something goes wrong, someone always pays a price." Who pays the price for things going wrong in this chapter? Make a list and explain your reasons for these choices.

14. What reasons did Vu give for so few gang members being in their thirties at the end of Chapter 14? Can you think of any other reasons this might be true?

15. In the beginning of Chapter 15, Vu says gang members have to move often. List some reasons why they might have to move. How might all these moves make life more difficult for Vu?

16. Why do you think Vu is beginning to ask himself questions throughout Part 3 of the book?

17. In Chapter 15, Vu wonders if God knows who he is. How does the Bible verse for this chapter relate to his concern?

18. In Chapter 18, what reason does Vu give for being a gang member? How does this compare to the reasons he gives in Chapter 9? Have his reasons changed over time? Explain your answer.

19. Why did Vu drive away from the man who stole his wallet in Chapter 20? How does the Bible verse help explain Vu's reaction? Do you think Vu would have driven away in Part 2 of his life's story?

20. What reason does Vu give in Chapter 21 for changing his name to Victor? Do you think this was a good idea? Explain your answer.

21. Why do Victor and Mylinh have three weddings?

22. What do you think Victor and his mother talked about when they were reunited?

23. In Chapter 23, what gift is Victor given from his father? Why does he feel his life has come "full circle?"

24. Why do you think Victor and Mylinh keep pictures of their deceased relatives in their living room?

25. What positive action does Victor take after his friend dies from a heroin overdose in Chapter 24?

26. If Victor does not like heights, why does he go sky diving? What message is Victor repeatedly giving to kids?

27. What reason is given in Chapter 24 for drug dealers offering free drugs to kids?

28. In the Postscript Bible verse, why is it not considered bragging to tell others of our good deeds?

29. What does Victor mean in the Postscript when he says, "I almost lost my life, but not my soul?"

PHOTO ALBUM

Vu's family in South Vietnam (Vu is boy on far right)

Mylinh and Victor's wedding in California

Victor and Mother in South Vietnam

Victor's Indiana MMA Hall of Fame induction with his father

Thank You God. Thank You Jesus.

Victor in front of VIP Nails

Victor's cars in front of VIP Nails

Victor with statue of Jesus and pictures of family
members in his living room

CPSIA information can be obtained
at www.ICGtesting.com
Printed in the USA
LVHW080032050121
675581LV00028B/604